HELPFUL PEOPLE

POLICE OFFICER

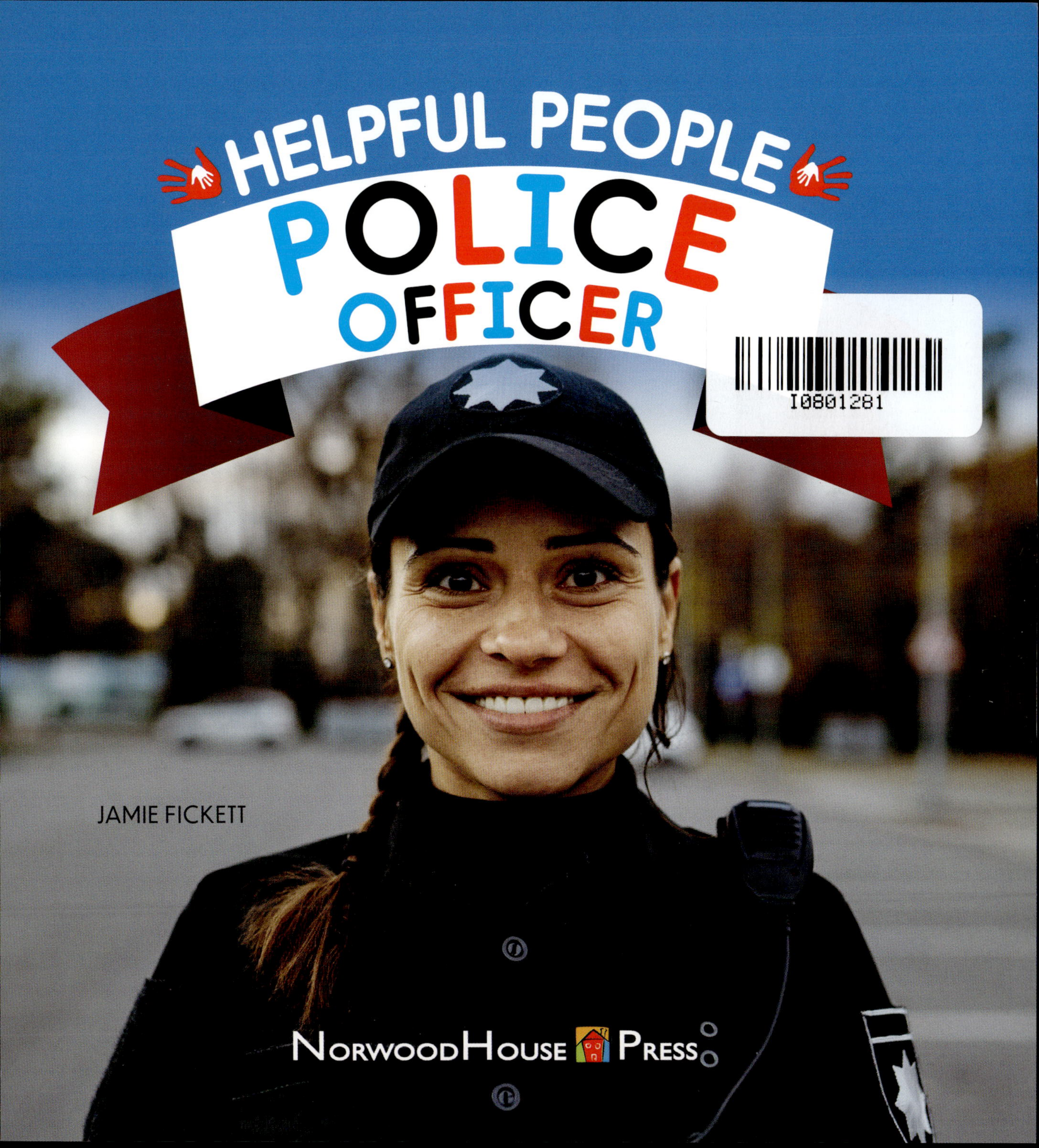

JAMIE FICKETT

NorwoodHouse Press

Library of Congress Cataloging-in-Publication Data:

Names: Fickett, Jamie.
Title: Police officer / Jamie Fickett.
Description: Buffalo, NY : Norwood House Press, 2025. | Series: Helpful people | Includes glossary and index.
Identifiers: ISBN 9781684503070 (pbk.) | ISBN 9781684503087 (library bound) | ISBN 9781684503094 (ebook)
Subjects: LCSH: Police--Juvenile literature.
Classification: LCC HV7922.F535 2025 | DDC 363.2--dc23

Published in 2025 by
Norwood House Press
2544 Clinton Street
Buffalo, NY 14224

Designer: Ocean Books
Editor: Kim Thompson

Photo credits: Cover, p. 1 Normad_Soul/Shutterstock.com; p. 5 Steve Sanchez Photos/Shutterstock.com; p. 6 Robert Kneschke/Shutterstock.com; p. 7 Alexander Oganezov/Shutterstock.com; p. 9 Ground Picture/Shutterstock.com; p. 11 Vaks-stock Agency/Shutterstock.com; p. 12 SchnepfDesign/Shutterstock.com; p. 13 Glynnis Jones; p. 15 Christian Mueller/Shutterstock.com; p. 16 Peopleimages.com/Shutterstock.com; p. 17 Ground Picture; p. 19 a Katz/Shutterstock.com; p. 21 Lightfield Studio

Printed in the United States of America

CPSIA compliance information: Batch #CW25NHP: For further information contact Norwood House Press at 1-800-237-9932.

TABLE OF CONTENTS

WHAT IS A POLICE OFFICER?

Police officers are important helpers in our **community**. They keep us safe and make sure everyone follows the law.

15025
BRATHWAITE
2084
SANTOS

Police officers **patrol** neighborhoods to watch for any trouble. When they see something wrong, they act quickly to fix the situation.

Police officers visit schools. They teach us how to stay safe and what to do in an **emergency**.

Police officers are friends to the community. They listen to people's problems and work to make things better.

WHAT DOES A POLICE OFFICER WEAR?

Police officers wear a special **uniform**. The shirt and pants are usually dark blue or black. The clothes have lots of pockets for carrying **tools**.

Police officers often wear a cap or a hat. It keeps the sun out of their eyes when they are outside.

A heavy belt called a duty belt is worn on the waist. It holds a radio, handcuffs, and a flashlight.

Police officers wear a shiny **badge** with a number. Patches on their uniforms might show the city they work in or their country's flag.

WHAT TOOLS DOES A POLICE OFFICER USE?

A police car is a tool that goes lightning fast. Flashing lights and loud sirens help police officers zoom through traffic.

NYPD
POLICE DOG KEEP BACK
COURTESY
PROFESSIONALISM
RESPECT

A radio lets police officers talk to each other. With the push of a button, they can give updates or get help.

Police officers also carry flashlights to help them see in dark places.

HOW DO YOU BECOME A POLICE OFFICER?

After finishing high school, police officers go to the **police academy**. They learn about laws and how to keep people safe.

When they finish the police academy, police officers take a big test. If they pass, they can get a badge and start working at a police station.

Good police officers are **brave**. They treat all people with respect. They are careful listeners who understand problems and how to solve them.

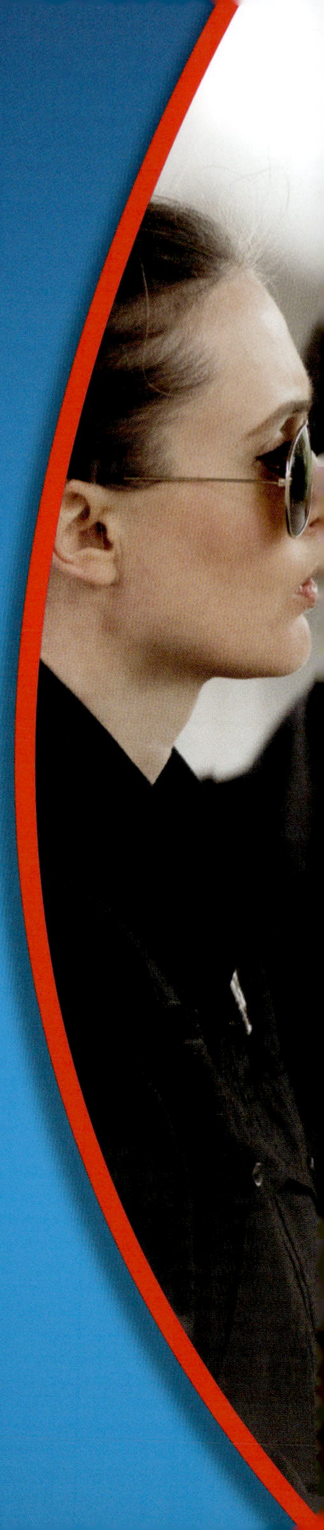

GLOSSARY

badge (baj): a small, flat object that you pin to your chest to show who you are or what you do

brave (brave): having the courage to do dangerous or risky things

community (kuh-MYOO-ni-tee): a social group of any size whose members live together, have a common government, and often share the same culture or history

emergency (i-MUR-juhn-see): a sudden and dangerous situation that requires immediate action

patrol (puh-TROHL): to travel around an area to watch it and to protect the people within it

police academy (puh-LEES uh-KAD-uh-mee): a school or college that provides special instruction and training for police officers

tools (toolz): pieces of equipment that you use to do a job; things that help you reach a goal

uniform (YOO-nuh-form): a special set of clothes worn by all members of a profession, organization, or rank

THINKING QUESTIONS

1. What is the job of a police officer?
2. Why does a police officer wear a belt?
3. How is a police officer helpful to the community?
4. What are the characteristics of a good police officer?
5. Would you like to become a police officer? Why or why not?

INDEX

ABOUT THE AUTHOR

Jamie Fickett lives on Long Island, New York, where he grew up. Every Saturday he enjoys going to the Bronx Zoo and seeing the rhinos from the Wild Asia Monorail. Rhinoceroses have been his favorite animal ever since he was eight and received the nickname Rhino while playing catcher in Little League baseball.